Crispin
Best

Hello

℈℈

PARTUS

Oxford · Reykjavík

MMXIX

First published in Great Britain in 2019 by Partus Press Ltd.

266 Banbury Road, Oxford OX2 7DL

www.partus.press

A CIP catalogue record for this book is available from the
British Library, ISBN 9781913196035

Designed in Oxford by Studio Lamont.

Printed & bound in Estonia.

CONTENTS

Thank you to the editors of *Pain*, *Prototype*, *Poems in Which*, *BODY*, *Faber New Poets 14* (Faber & Faber, 2016), *I Love Roses When They're Past Their Best*, and *Queen Mob's Tea House*, in which some of these poems previously appeared. 'io' was performed at the Serpentine Gallery as part of the 89+ Marathon. 'poem in which i mention at the last moment an orrery' adapts some lines about herons from Donald Revell's poem 'A Branch of the Discipline', from his collection *There Are Three* (Wesleyan University Press, 1998).

Thanks to Rebecca Perry, Kathryn Maris, Vala Thorodds, Luke Allan, Amy Key, Sam Riviere, Sarah Jean Alexander, Ginny, Martha Sprackland, Rachael Allen, Ricardo Domeneck, Vlad Pojoga, Cătălina Stanislav, Lucy K. Shaw, Bongo, Emily Berry, Heather Phillipson, Jane Yeh, Eleanor Chandler, Richard Scott, Jack Underwood, Wayne Holloway-Smith, Alex MacDonald, Michael Inscoe, Meggie Green, Louise, Stacey Teague, Natalie Chin, Matthew Riviere, Megan Nolan, Rachel Benson, Ben Brooks, and, I'm sure, many others. And to you, for this.

i love it when cows eat the floor
and if you let yourself
it can almost hurt
to wonder where a helicopter went

i know in my heart that i'm a cowboy
i know that i'm here to try to help
put your bad fortune back inside the cookie

i know that i'm here for the moment
that the pickles hit the plate
i'm here for good and to pair your socks
by windowlight

and to the man who told me there is too much me
in my poems
hello

while i have my first
snowball fight of the year
i want to tell you
that the moon
is my favourite kind
of indirect light

i throw a tiny snowball
and watch you catch it
in your mouth and no-one
has leaned over and kissed me
in a long time

you ask if i know
that the reason it's called gravy is because
eventually
you die

all i know
is that looking
at the dark slice of the moon
is looking at light that hit the earth
first
then came back

i throw a snowball directly up
and close my eyes

earthlight

the last time someone kissed me
i could feel their mouth smiling
and i don't know if that is good

but tonight i am a power station
in your countryside
and on a scale of alive
we are alive

here is the thing:
the real reason i don't let people
get close to me
is this faux denim shirt
i'm scared that
they will be able to tell

einstein said
his second best idea
was to boil an egg
in his soup as it cooked
frankly i get halfway through a sentence
and want to break a tennis racket

at the dinner table
i ask for your thoughts on wind turbines
'big fan' you say
we try not to laugh
and through the window
look at the bad clouds
being bad and
the good clouds
being clouds

here is the thing:
there are even tiny movements
of your fingers
that i don't
completely understand

frankly i get halfway
through a poem
and it's nearly night
the same sunset
has been travelling
around the earth
for millions of years

it is good to be talked to
and also
to hear people sleep

here is the thing:
between the boiler's ticks
i hear you whisper
that you had a hunch
about the shirt

from this great distance
i make my arms the perfect length

caring about a person
is like asking a bagel
how to live

barack obama what should i do
with my only life
what if v neck stood for
very neck

at every turn
people find things quite unbelievable
every cat has a dad
take a moment now barack
to consider the implications

inviting a person to care about you is like
telling them 'take a seat'
and pointing at a month-old pretzel

there is a music to burying things
barack there is even something
unbearable about escalators
if you need there to be

i admit i often want to tell a sunrise 'whoa'
like it is drunk and trying to fight

i laugh at the sheer
machinery of feelings barack
with all my doors expanded
in their frames

a custard pie in the face
of certain death

barack it might be enough just to find
a longer hair in my sink
once in a while

caring about a person is like
praying to a doughnut in the dark

still though barack
still my only life

again and again the grass fills this useless space
between the ground and the air

and again

ONE GOOD THING

the ceiling fan just lives there
i touch your back
while the sun does
and later on the empty bus home
roll off the seat when we corner too fast

and stay on the floor
for a moment thinking
one good thing
about being alive
is the view

DON'T CALL IT A DREAM

i let summer take over the house
for however long it needs
and what is it
about the clawed opening of dawn
that makes me want to call it that

if you can't do the crime
don't do the crime
and don't thank me for the birthday wishes
please
just let me grow my beans

TO BE HONEST

so often it is the part of the night
when the pizza is slowly burning
i love this time of day
the same way
i like the backs of statues best

to be honest
sometimes i do make
a little anguished noise
as i pull on my shoes
and sometimes as i open the curtain
a single bird will fly from the tree

but today the knee of a thought
will crumple beneath me
again and again
i will sit softly
on the lip of a mattress
hoping only not to harm it
and today i will try again
tomorrow

HOW GOOD

in my room
through whatever windows we can find
all the sun that we can see
is setting
like a table

it isn't barbecue weather but
even that won't stop
some people

i feel good like a person
holding flowers on a train
feels dumb

in my room
you tell me
that the hole in my pocket
is just my pocket's own
much larger pocket
and i feel good
like burying a spade

like stapling a tree's leaves back onto it
is bad

like holy water
on a hedgehog's back

every decision we make
is a vote we are casting
for the type of world in which
we want to live
i say this
and you frown
and i feel good
like the stains on your sleeve
wherever you care
to have made them

like the space station
its various randy astronauts
making their way from meal to meal
across the sky

i feel good
but how good can we even feel
in a world where thunder and lightning
are back to front
where more time now won't mean
less eternity later

how good can we even feel
when any minute
our life together could be ruined
by imagining a lobster
wearing jeans

there is an outside
which is everywhere we aren't
and through whatever windows
we can find
the sun has set
like an alarm

i look at you with my finger
in my pocket's pocket

things are obvious
once you know

..
.....
....
....
....
....
....
....
....
....
....
....
....
....
.....picture me wearing a t-shirt.........
....
....that says...
....
...............'you are the universe's way................
....
....
.............................of observing itself'......................
....
....

....

....

....

....

....

.................and what if books.............................

....

...................were eggs...............................

....

.............a library..................................

....

....

....

....

.................would just be a building.....................

....

....

....full.....................

....

....

....of eggs.....

....

....

....

....

....

....

....

....

....

..........what about a t-shirt that says..........................

....

...............................'happiness is a destination..........

....

....

..............only in the way..

....that a hovercraft is'..........

....

....

....

....

....

....becky.....

....

.....................great photo......................

....

.....................of you with your......................

....

....

....

....

..........jukebox...

....

....

....

....

....

....

...................do they even have the ocean.......

....

....in heaven...

....

....

...................do they even.................................

....

....

....

....

....have heaven..................

....

....

....in heaven...

....

....

....

....

....

....

....

....

....

...........picture the kid who thinks...........

...........the reason to stay away...........

...........from the window...........

...........during a tornado...........

...........is in case...........

...........the tornado sees you...........

....

....

....

.........picture low sunlight strobing through the railings....

....

....

.................as we walk..

....

....

....

....

...................becky..

....

.......................you are older than i remember......

....

....

....

....

....

.............don't talk to the hat..................................

....

....

....

....

.......................talk to the thing.....................

....

....

....

....under the hat...............

....

....

....

....

....

....

....

....

....

....

....

............today we're going to talk about.........................

....

....

....

...............................how it feels to be.....................

....

....

....

....

....

....

...............how even a low moon.....................................

....

....

....

..............can paint a bridge on a lake.................

....

....

....

....

....

...........how if you feel an urge to work...........................

....

.........................take a nap and it will pass.................

....

....

....

....

....

....................how i love the wind.......................

....

....

....

.................when it brings your clothes to life..........

....

....

....

..........picture a passion fruit...........

......................why is it called that name...

..........my only kink...........

............is having my clothes blown off..............

..........................by a leaf blower..........

......and the best part of any sandwich................

......................is all of it..........

....

............it is true that the sun...........

....

....

...........makes the darkness rise..................

....

......................the shadows..........................

....

....

..................speak to the light..........................

....

..................................and so on...................

....

....

....

....

....

....

.....cold air batters my twig......................

....

....

..................................on the beach.....

....

....

....

....
...........................picture cats.............................
....
....
...................as god's security cameras.................
....
....
....
....
....
....
....
....
....
....
....
....
....
....
....
....
....
....
....
....

....

....

....

....

....

....

....

....

....

....

....

....

....

....

....

....

....

....

....

....

....

....

....what if cum is ghosts............

....

....

....

....

....

....

....

....

....

....

....picture yourself warping...

....

........................in the window display....................

....

....

....

....

....

...........and what's more...

....

............part of me always wants...................................

....

...........................to throw a salad off a roof...........

....

....

....

....

........................it is often that a person's mouth...........

....

....

....

....
....breaks their nose.............

....

....

....
.............that a person's mouth.......................................
.................breaks their heart.......................................

....

....
....and so on...

....

....

....

....

....
...........picture someone waving to us from land.......

....

....
........while we are on a boat..

....

....

....

....

....

....

....

....

....

....

.............how are existing...

....

......................................and not existing.........................

....

....

....

....

.............................the only two options.............

....

....

....

....

........picture walking into the wall in mcdonald's............

....

...................and saying...

....

...........................'out of my way, mcdonald's'..........

....

....

....

............................and walking into the wall.............

....

....

....

....
....again.............................

....

....

....

....

....

....

....

....

.........................my only kink...............................

....

....

.........................is holding hands....................

....

....

....while my phone charges...

....

....

....

....

.........picture a peacock...

....

....

............................putting sunlight all over himself....

....

....

....
....
....
.............i like things like....................................
....
....
...............how fast you climb the stairs................
....
....
....
.............like how werewolves.....................
....
.............don't kill people.....................
....
....
....
....
....
....
.............................full moons do.........
....
....
....
....
....
....
....

..................like how..

....

....

............you can just.....................................

....

....

..........wear a pair..

....

..............................of trousers...................

....

....

....

........and people will assume...........................

....

....

............................they are.......................

....

....

....

....

....

....your trousers.......

....

....

....

....

....

....

....

....

....

....

....

...............centralia...........

....

....

....

....

....

.........a lead balloon..

....

....

...........................actually goes down......................

....

....pretty well.....

....

....

....

....

....

....

....

....

40

....

....

....

...........people with beards...

....

....

....

....

....

....are just people without beards.......

....

....

....

....

....

....

....

....

....

....

....

....

....with beards.............

....

....

....

increasingly
i regret things
in the sun
i acknowledge
and regret things
in the sun
i dream less often
of having a dog
i have access
to fewer emotions
in the sun
and i long for a poem
that is just about
i don't know
cucumbers
it is too easy
to always be ashamed
music is different
in zoos
music is different
in the sun
i like the word
fireplace
and want

to bite through
the porcelain
of a mug
while you watch
increasingly
when dancing
i think only
of fingers lost
to ceiling fans
or else
pity the people
who think
that the room is there
to make eye contact
across
how do we feel
and how do we feel
in the sun
i like the word
skyline
and one
of the many things
i acknowledge is
no one ever
called me a flute
and blew in my ear
but increasingly

i live less
 in the world
 and want nothing
  more from it
   than a poem about
    cucumbers
     that have been
      left alone
        to be their gentle selves
        in the sun
         it is my talent
          that is modest
          not me

POEM IN WHICH I MENTION AT THE LAST MOMENT
AN ORRERY

there are certain
people i have only ever met in
the rain

i am a moon and you
are a moon
i mean i am the moon and yes
you are too
i am calmer when we're the
moon if you can believe such
a thing

consider the things my body is
for example there is a part of it
which is an ankle
another part which i can only describe as
the distance between distance
and distance
a part which makes a muffled
hopeful noise and another part which is
an ankle

on the moon there is an american flag
on us though there is nothing
just now

of the 47 nesting herons
displaced by the recent storm
47 died

i have stopped doing the thing you sometimes
complain about
which we notice at the same time
tapioca exists you've just
remembered and so tell me

oh my heavens we think and then
the word tapioca
together

moon and moon
tapioca

all the same there are certain people
i have never met

good morning pop music
is inside me like a wind

pop music is in me like
gas in the moon

there is an orrery
of us
i have seen it behind
glass and it is true

DON'T WORRY

if you find yourself downwind from the fountain
don't worry
when you die you just
become a children's magician
and in fact relax

ghosts don't kill people
because imagine how awkward it would be afterwards
don't worry
not even in the fountain spray
with everywhere the rude dispersal of light

I CAN CHANGE

i love it when my business is transformed
and i am in a hammock and the wind
and it is morning
i don't know
somewhere

a phone glinting
with what i hope is no information
a swan of sound approaching on the lake
in terms of the things i'm trying to say
i'm not

in berlin
a man laughs at my legs
and i feel almost put here
to someday leave a grapefruit
on your doorstep at night

laughing thinking
how sad of an emperor is a heart

in a tiny rowboat
i feel almost put here
to puff out my chest
at the other tiny rowboats

in berlin
a man laughs at my legs
on the train

in berlin
i look at you
i like both of your hats

i feel almost put here
to hold my horses

to laugh thinking
how sad of an emperor
is a heart

in berlin
i watch my clothes slowly die

in parks we are confused
by the grass
what does it want from us

i feel almost put here
to climb through your window giggling
and knock over your toiletries

should anything happen to me in berlin
will you want my body

you pulled a cherry blossom
off the tree again

should anything happen to me in berlin
please live forever

i lean on the lamp post
and wait

aloha from hell

how sad of an emperor
we all are eventually

haha

WHO ELSE

i tell the same stories
again and again
because who else is going to
and what are the builders making

apart from a racket
the black mould in my room makes it feel
like the wall is learning something

i tell my computer i'm not a robot
when it asks
because who else is going to

i can't believe you thanked me
for sleeping in your bed

if a tree falls in the forest
that's fine

MY GOD

you have no idea
of the distances i would travel
just to disappoint you

i will even wear a fashionable shoe
my god
just watch me

another? i ask
go ahead you say

and another?

no that's too many shoes

we shout
we throw bits of the forest at the forest
we walk

the so-called trees and the sky
a so-called kite and a cloud
my god
the so-called sky but first the trees

if you hold my hand
hold my hand
it could even rain

a walk in the wet leaves

my so-called shoe comes off in the mud

my god these yellow socks

i love them

NATURE POEM

we're here
i'm alone with you in capital letters

through the window a tall crane builds new things far away

we're here
i hit the lampshade with a towel
dust and dead mosquitos fall
and us here in all of it

realise that part of me
is already haunting every mcdonald's i've ever been in
and part of you
is already haunting every place you've ever kissed me
yes you are haunting my collarbone

we're here
you are like a tulip when there are tulips behind you and i
    can't decide what you're like
yes you are haunting my kneebacks
yes you are haunting my chest through my t-shirt at night
yes you are haunting all 360° of a rickety ferris wheel

we're here
realise that at every moment you're the only visible part of
    an almost infinite conga line
ok now imagine crying while wearing cargo shorts
it's hard to do

tonight we share a rocking chair
toothpaste
this blue-orange night sky

i'm alone with you with a crane in the distance
congratulations
tonight our lives will change 0% in every direction

so let's move to the country
you can grow back your eyebrows
and i can wear a vest for the first time
and you can point at a chicken and laugh
and i can punch a flower and it is ok
and you can say the most interesting thing about me is that
    i like you so much
and i can put my body high up in a tree and wait
and you can thank me for all the butterflies we saw today
and i can say 'you are all of the butterflies' as you try to count
and you can cry dreaming that we had a baby and i made
    you dress her in one ugg and one croc

and i can look at you pointing at a chicken and laughing and
    point at a chicken and laugh with you
and you can hold a tiny leaf and say 'leaflet'
and i can listen to a crow talk and it is beautiful music
and you can fall in love with quiet forest water noises in this
    forest
and i can like animals and you are one
and you can look at our knees and feet all in the grass while
    i sleep
and i can touch a mushroom and imagine being a mushroom
and you can shout that you think you saw a fish
and i can say 'this is my only life these are my only teeth'
and you can say 'this is your only knee' and kick me in the
    knee
and i can push hard on the west side of a tree and you're
    welcome i'm turning planet earth
and you can see a quiet frog looking up at a nebula and it is
    an excellent beast
and i can wear the heck out of some scarves with you
and you can wear the heck out of some scarves with me
and i can smile watching mist be mist
and you can put bad dark berries near your lips and then on
    the ground instead
and i can blink watching lightning connect a sycamore to a
    sky
and you can stab a bonfire with a branch and think 'yes sir i
    am hurting this fire'

and i can put my body high up in a tree and wait

and you can tell me 'don't worry your sadness isn't going
anywhere let's just be alright together awhile'

and i can get drunk and touch your ribs a lot while you are
trying to sleep

and you can brush my teeth for me

and i can smile as my gums are bleeding in our two-man tent

and you can put your hand around my bare wrist and say
'i hate your bracelet'

and i can look at geese and wow they are so very geese in
the rain

and you can cry missing belgian buns

and i can be a tourist in so much of you

and bugs will find us again and again

we will wear bugs at night

and bugs will wear us too

THIS IS HOW

i

saw

a

sad

person

on

the

morning

train

a

sad

person

on

a

lounger

beside

a

rooftop

swimming

pool

another

sad

person

in
a
safari
park
with
the
hyenas
some
people
have
expensive
umbrellas
and
are
still
sad
i
go
to
work
on
the
morning
train
and
i

am
brave
though
it
is
true
that
i
can
come
home
and
make
myself
a
sandwich
by
putting
a
slice
of
bread
on
either
side
of

my
face
birds
have
no
idea
what
they
are
doing
and
this
is
how
i
am
like
birds

in my dream
i found out that my dad
was a wheelie bin
and i hugged the wheelie bin
and my mum said
'not that wheelie bin'
but i stayed hugging it

i have been thinking
about the time the universe
was the size of a cantaloupe

oh my

there are things i have
been confused about

there are things about which
i have been confused

when i asked if things are serious
with your new boyfriend
did you say you are just dating
or gestating

i wish for you pancakes
a wicker fence
a cat bewildered
bells in the distance
a cat in heat trying
to flirt with a wicker fence
i wish for you bells

i have crushed cans
while thinking of you

i have also cradled
a croissant
like a baby
so

i wish for you sirens going off like milk
i wish for you the evening
foxes sneezing in the streets below
the night

i wish for you butterflies in the airport

i have been thinking of the universe
it never gets older when i read how old it is
the sun paints me brightly
polishes the daymoon

above my head
oh my

i wish for you a warm balcony
to own at least one loveseat in your lifetime
the most beautiful waitress
i wish for you a bird screaming on a church roof
while you are trying to sleep

dusk is a good word to say during dusk

i wish for you
my heart is beating like a whisk

i wish for you birds
to find an uninflated balloon in your pocket
i wish for you the perfect banana
bluebirds for youbirds
a person waving down from the fifteenth floor excited
cows
birds

cows

i have been thinking about the universe
even distant fireworks
make me think of the people who lit them

i can't help it

the builders are building a building

i will be honest
the animal does not understand
that you are photographing him

i wish for you the ocean when you least
expect it

fast running is good
i wish i could do it

WHAT DO I KNOW

i love it when poems
are dead
and the light
creeps under the door
and not too far away
something important
is about to be crushed
by that beautiful truck

or when poems are dead
and a blade of shadow
wipes itself across the yard
with the nettles as strange
as you want them to be
when they worry your legs
i love that too

almost nothing
is any of my business
and i wish even less was

i brush my teeth
like i hate them

at last
poems are dead
but what do i know

all i know is that
no child should ever have to wear
a bib that claims they are
the world's best anything

all i do is gun fingers
at a moth
in the dark
and what can i say
at least we have given up
completely this time

i love it when that happens

INTEL

we're playing the intel jingle
on your parents' piano again
adding octaves
and getting louder each time
i'm screaming and smiling
and you are smiling

are moths weird or am i

we stop
i pet your head and say
'we stopped'
and
'that's ok'

imagine a dog that could open a patio door
that's me for you

i feel like
do leaf insects know other leaf insects aren't just leaves
and
it's late

BUT DO DOLPHINS WANT

TO SWIM WITH ME

in the morning / i sing alarm clocks / in the shower / and think about work / about how a towel is just a big napkin / for my body / how shampoo is just the way / i put ether in my hair / i hang my big napkin naked by the window / and look out at the world / men are dangerous / and weak / if you go to another country / you will be left alone there / too

however hard i try / i can't imagine / calling a bonfire mine /
and every failure hits me / like a tunnel of bricks / still / the
good news is / if not used / my phone can live / sometimes
for days / the bad news / is i am not here / to teach a lesson /
i would simply like / to offer my finger / and for someone to
bite / today was the birthday / of a friend / of a friend / i saw
the cake

the cooking apples / have long gone brown / on the countertop / nights arrive like iguanas in suits / and with them the long dream / on a beach / where a pop-up notification / blocks the sunset / these poems are the kiddie pools / i inflate while i'm alive today in the street / i either saw / a man dressed as a chef / or a chef / and in quieter moments / remember that german has a word / for what caged birds feel / in migration season / that the internet / is just an internet cafe / without the cafe / that the only thing wrong / is your expectations / mother nature / witness how my enemies shed my blood

i just called to tell you / that my home is uninsured / that i
feel strong / like how dandruff has a strength / that you have
never been / in an empty room / that sometimes i have no
idea / what time it is / and to ask you / why would a person
ruin a place / by jogging through it / may your bike fly into
heaven / blessed be

a fierce look from a graveyard duck / can be enough / a single astonishing lime / can turn a rotten morning / on its head / an abandoned mattress might seem enough / since it means a junior ghost / has finally earned its sheet / some days though / don't even feel like days / our hands / in gloves / curl up you don't have to believe in doors / or that technically all worms are earth worms / you don't have to believe in / a massage so good / that it will make you glad / you have a body / or that the next time you won't be terrified of death / you'll be dead / that of all the available beards / still sometimes the goatee is chosen / you don't even have to believe / that anteaters exist / but let's at least agree / that although cottage pie is a strange name / shepherd's is the saddest pie because / look / he is eating / his friends i give myself away / like crisps / and even the compliments i pay / reveal the things / i hate / i long to hang glide / with a thud / into the face / of that perfect cliff / the shame / of just going about / my idiot business / from day to idiot day / sticks to me / like a dark sausage always / how can i be expected / to live in a world / where a one-way mirror / is also known as / a two-way mirror i tell myself / the bananas i eat / are allergic to me / i go away / and bring back / dirty clothes / and could never hide / in the bathroom / since there's no one / to hide from / experience is something you get / moments after you need it / there is no more to say / i may continue to affect things / for a while after i'm gone

YOUR INBOX GENTLY FILLS

this hospital
could use a hospital you think
while the world feels big and spooky again
and back at home
your inbox gently fills

it's not quite true
that every car should stop
while a poem is in operation
but try to tell me
it wouldn't be nice

i still hate walking through the long grass
startling the sheep as the train slams by
i hate when a staircase leads only to a ceiling
the way tractors act
we store things almost forever
i hate that dead space
between your mattress and the floor
how the light fades
i hate the longing for objects
how backpacks follow me around creepily
that there is a me inside me
who sets alarms
the sounds of baby birds
when i can't see them
or geese when i've given up
i hate not knowing what to do
with good old death
teaching oneself one's flaws are virtues
glitter glue on bald spots and so on
what even is there to say about fish
i hate frowning at coleslaw
and that the secret to my success
is just that i'm in bed and drunk

increasingly i hate
that i don't even need to be looked at
that the object of golf
is to play as little golf
as possible

i am nearer to a fax than i have ever been before

and just think
next time we are together
hundreds of people will be sleeping in submarines somewhere

why wouldn't they

so watch me minimise firefox sitting in a swivel chair for you
bent and straightened beside the water cooler
eating soup at my desk at my desk
my doleful finger in so much phone cord

i would even bother the folds of your shucked-off
    undergarment
listen i would literally wear a white sweater in an office if
    i had to

if i smile when i say
'these doors are alarmed?
why what's happened?'
i'm sorry
i am most beautiful while printing out emails
and yes when i think of you i am hard at work

you are the reason i'm looking round at a brainstorm
thinking
what right now are the different ways i can hurt myself

six minutes wild texting in a toilet cubicle
you are the reason for watching bowls rotate in microwaves
brewing cups of tea by windowlight

your email says italic text is named for the tower of pisa
while i see words leaning into a cold wind

i'm shredding ancient contracts in conditioned air for you

hello glass meeting room table i'm falling through you now
what if i just started eating the plants
the strings that control these blinds might take my weight
at the neck

quiet
here look i am
fluorescing

when i die
stomp 3,000 alabaster skateboards
in my memory
kickflip my corpse
into a ditch
eat pizza
sing

when i'm alive
i am dropping a frisbee
with everyone watching
if we ever talk
and you don't smile

there are hills in you and i am on them

o greyskull
o solemn wall-hung portrait of a kangaroo
o digestive biscuits in the spring

there are hills i am on

i love you is like sitting on a bench

when i die
remember us
it's cold
i can only hug your legs one way
and they can only hug me another
i like both

i am beside myself when i am beside myself
i am beside myself when i am beside you

o goatse in the snow
o tubgirl in the rain
o modern american poetry

the trees outside are covered with
outside
thank you for telling me you're pregnant
and i'm the baby

on uranus a year lasts 84 years

o besunglassed sun in the summer
o party rings
o life
o des'ree
o sonique

on uranus you die on your first birthday

when i'm alive
feed me ex boyfriends' foibles
your thoughts on films
past moral lapses
let me be your ginger hard drive

o dragostea din tea
o thudding in the electric lumber of my chest
o fisher price
o fiddlesticks

motherfucking teresa
i think of you while eating peanuts

o brookside
o blobby
o burmese cliffbuilt monastery in may

i want you on google street view

my big idea
is basically just the xgames
but for dogs

o bison
o balrog
o blanka
o guile

by the way
i've never kissed someone
this close to a plug socket
before
thank you

o earthquake
o savage
o hitman
o hulk

when i'm alive
it is strange
to be naked in one room
and then walk to another room
and be naked there
instead

we have raised this wild invisible animal
alone together
came home to it
what did we expect

when i die
know that i died how i lived:
not wanting to die

scatter my ashes on the internet

we have made it to the wildflowers again
throw your socks into the distance
you are the barefoot me

o haunted toaster buried in a panic and the woods
o kerplunk
o puzz 3-d
o cloud cap over mount cleveland

riot of colour of io

when i die
roll my body down an up-escalator
i feel like my skeleton might enjoy that
eventually

pluto has a heart-shaped sea
that's filled with poisonous ice
so let's watch cool runnings in the bath
sitting like they do

o distance
o crystal maze
o gentle choad poking meekly out
o blue corn tortilla on the ground

when i'm alive
find me shirtless
in your dreams
screaming i love you
like white people love mambo #5
whispering i love you
like a bike

we like each other and vice versa

o curly wurly wrapper
o nokia 3210
o crepitating autumn leaf
o mars bar ice cream in september and the rain

if you read this your life will be better
let's go bowling to celebrate
it's friday with you even when it isn't

especially

I'M NOT LATE

i'm not late
i'm just walking fast
and i hope the two distant saxophones
know about one another

i want you
to understand
that it isn't an oven
it's a pizza machine

this grudging agreement
follows me everywhere
and i raise eyebrows
as if they were my own

when the sun catches me
i catch the sun
when you break a net
it has fewer holes

sometimes i look at a mouse
and sometimes i know
exactly how many mountains
should appear all at once

whatever depths there are
are better plumbed by someone else
but when we saw that chameleon
being born

we screamed